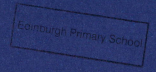

REAL WORLD DATA

GRAPHING SPORT

Casey Rand

www.heinemannlibrary.co.uk
Visit our website to find out more information about Heinemann Library books.

To order:
☎ Phone +44 (0) 1865 888066
🖨 Fax +44 (0) 1865 314091
💻 Visit www.heinemannlibrary.co.uk

Heinemann Library is an imprint of Capstone Global Library Limited, a company incorporated in England and Wales having its registered office at 7 Pilgrim Street, London, EC4V 6LB – Registered company number: 6695582

"Heinemann" is a registered trademark of Pearson Education Limited, under licence to Capstone Global Library Limited

Edited by Megan Cotugno and Diyan Leake
Designed by Victoria Bevan and Geoff Ward
Original illustrations © Capstone Global Library Ltd 2010
Illustrated by Geoff Ward
Picture research by Mica Brancic, Q2AMedia
Originated by Chroma Graphics (Overseas) Pte Ltd
Printed in China by Leo Paper Products Ltd

ISBN 978 0 431033 47 1 (hardback)
14 13 12 11 10
10 9 8 7 6 5 4 3 2 1

British Library Cataloguing in Publication Data
Rand, Casey
Graphing sport. – (Real world data)
796'.0728-dc22
A full catalogue record for this book is available from the British Library.

Acknowledgements
We would like to thank the following for permission to reproduce photographs: Corbis pp. **4** (Libon of Elis), **6** (Ben Radford), **8** (Erich Schlegel), **11** (Paul J. Sutton), **12** (Bettmann), **20** (Jeff Zelevansky), **24** (Bob Krist), **26** (Clifford White); Dreamstime p. **14**; EPA p. **16** (Daniel Dal Zennaro); Photolibrary p. **18** (Crow Hufton); Reuters p. **10** (Shaun Best); Shutterstock p. **22** (Chen Wei Seng).

Cover photograph of David Oliver of the United States in the men's 110m hurdles heats at the 2008 Olympic Games in Beijing, China, reproduced with permission of Getty Images (Bongarts/Alexander Hassenstein).

We would like to thank Lou Amodeo for his invaluable help in the preparation of this book.

Every effort has been made to contact copyright holders of any material reproduced in this book. Any omissions will be rectified in subsequent printings if notice is given to the publisher.

CONTENTS

Some words are printed in bold, **like this**. You can find out what they mean by looking in the glossary, on page 30.

Look around you! Sport is on television, the radio, and the Internet. Sport takes place in the water, on the snow, and in the sky. Sport is enjoyed by many people – children, adults, and even some animals participate in sport!

The birth of sport

The first written records of sporting events are thousands of years old. However, sport has been played even longer than this. Cave drawings from 30,000 years ago have been found showing sporting events. Early sports were different from those played now but some involved running, kicking, and throwing, just like many sports today.

The first Olympic Games took place in ancient Greece in 776 BCE. They were held in a place called Olympia.

Sport today

Sports have changed a lot since the time of cave drawings and ancient Greece. Modern technologies, such as television and radio, have made sport more popular than ever. Sports stars have become big celebrities and some make millions of pounds! Still, like in ancient times, sport can be played by anyone and can be good entertainment and great exercise for everyone.

The Temple of Zeus in Olympia was a site of early Olympic games.

Tables, graphs, and timelines

A graph can be used to display the information from a table in a way that is easy to read. The timeline below is a type of graph. It takes each point from the table and shows it in a different way. It makes seeing and understanding the order of Olympic events much easier.

What happened?	When?
IOC (International Olympic Committee) is formed	1894
Athens Games: first modern Olympics	1896
Women allowed to compete for first time	1900
Olympics cancelled due to World War I	1916
First televised Olympics	1936
First of two Olympics cancelled due to World War II	1940
Muhammad Ali wins gold in boxing	1960
First use of artificial snow at Olympics	1980
Snowboarding becomes Olympic sport	1998
2008 Beijing games: most watched Olympics ever	2008

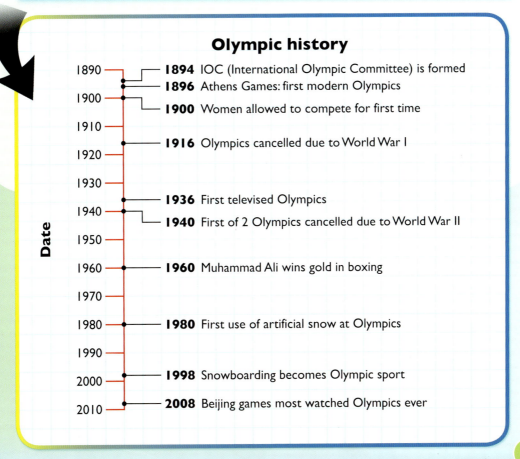

Olympic history

Date

- **1894** IOC (International Olympic Committee) is formed
- **1896** Athens Games: first modern Olympics
- **1900** Women allowed to compete for first time
- **1916** Olympics cancelled due to World War I
- **1936** First televised Olympics
- **1940** First of 2 Olympics cancelled due to World War II
- **1960** Muhammad Ali wins gold in boxing
- **1980** First use of artificial snow at Olympics
- **1998** Snowboarding becomes Olympic sport
- **2008** Beijing games most watched Olympics ever

The ancient Romans played a game like football but with more players. Games very similar to football were played nearly 3,000 years ago in Japan and China. Today it is the world's most played, most watched, and most popular sport.

Banned!

Football has not always been accepted worldwide. In a period of time spanning from the 14th to 17th centuries, rulers in parts of Europe – England, particularly – actually passed laws banning the sport. In the 14th century, King Edward II was so appalled by the game, he made playing football illegal anywhere in the country. Those that broke the law faced possible imprisonment.

Football stars

Football has come a long way since being forbidden. Overall, there are probably over a billion footballers on the planet today. The best players are famous all over the world.

David Beckham is a **midfielder** who has played for Manchester United, Real Madrid, Los Angeles Galaxy, and AC Milan. He was captain of England for six years and is one of the most popular players of all time!

Pelé

Edson Arantes do Nascimento, more famously known as Pelé, is a Brazilian considered to be one of the greatest footballers ever. He is the only player to be part of three **World Cup**-winning teams. People all over the world admired him. He could even stop wars! In 1967 the two sides of the Nigerian Civil War actually agreed to a 48-hour ceasefire so they could watch Pelé play!

Line graphs

A line graph is a graph that can be used to show how things change over time. In this line graph, we can see how David Beckham's goal scoring has changed over time. Each point on the graph represents the number of goals Beckham scored each year. A line connects each point so we can see how his scoring changed year to year. Can you tell how many goals Beckham scored in his 10th year?

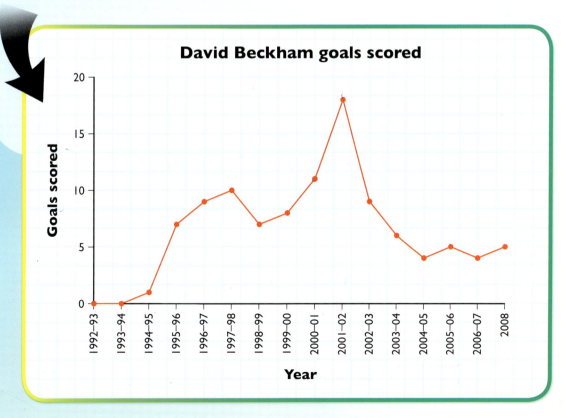

David Beckham goals scored

TRACK AND FIELD

The ancient Olympic Games were mainly made up of running events. In the Olympics today, running, jumping, and throwing events are grouped into a collection known as **track and field**.

Blazing speeds

The running races in track and field include short, medium, and long distances. Some of the races include barriers that the runners have to jump over! These barriers are called hurdles. The winner of the 100-metre race at international competitions is often considered the world's fastest man or woman.

Super strength

Track and field also includes events where the participants must pick up an object and throw it as far as they can. These events include the javelin, hammer, discus, and shot put. Athletes in these events use their strength to put lots of force into their throws. The men's shot put weighs 7.26 kilograms (16 pounds) and the women's weighs 4 kilograms (8 pounds). The men's world record for the shot put is over 23 metres (75 feet). The longest throw by a woman is over 22 metres (72 feet).

 An Olympic javelin throw may travel over 90 metres (300 feet).

Long leaps

The high jump, long jump, and pole vault are all track and field events. In the pole vault, participants use a long, flexible pole to catapult themselves as high as possible over a bar. The women's world record for the pole vault is over 5 metres (16 feet).

The world's fastest man

The line graph below shows the times recorded over the years for the Olympic gold, silver, and bronze winners in the men's Olympic 100-metre race. The **x-axis** (which runs left to right across the page) shows some of the years in which the Summer Olympics were held. The **y-axis** (which runs up and down the page) shows the time in seconds in which the medalists finished for each of the years on the x-axis.

In 1936 American track star Jesse Owens won the gold medal. In 2008 Jamaican track star Usain Bolt won the gold medal. Can you tell who would have won in a race between Owens and Bolt?

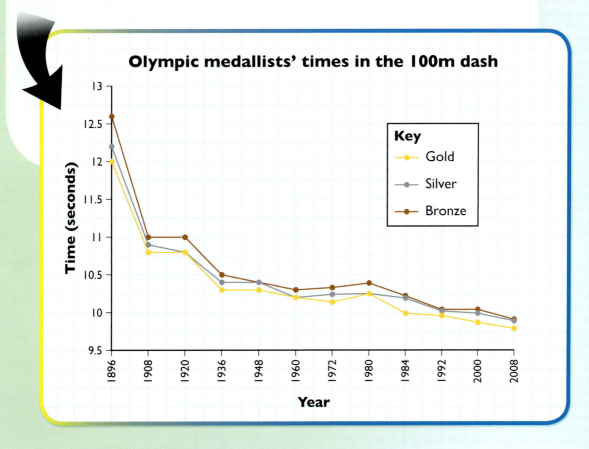

Olympic medallists' times in the 100m dash

The track and field are not the only locations where sport takes place. There are many sports that take place in the water.

Football in water?

Water polo is a sport that is similar to football. There are two teams each with six field players and one goalkeeper. Each team tries to score goals by getting a ball into the net past the other team's goalkeeper. The biggest difference between water polo and football is that water polo is played in water! All players in water polo are also allowed to use their hands to pass and shoot the ball.

Active and fit

Many more sports take place in the water including swimming, diving, and rowing. Water sports can be great exercise. Swimming can actually burn more calories per hour than running.

Super swimmers

Chris Holmes is considered to be one of the greatest paralympic swimmers of all time. Holmes is a British swimmer who won nine gold medals despite being partially sighted. (He is blind in one eye and can see only a little with the other eye.)

Britain's youngest ever Paralympic gold medal winner is swimmer Eleanor Simmonds. In 2008 she won two gold medals at the age of only 13. Her second medal came in world-record time.

Water polo is the football of the swimming pool.

2008 Olympic 100-metre butterfly

The scale of a graph determines how much detail we can see. The first graph below breaks down the 100-metre butterfly into a scale of 2 metres on the x-axis and 1 second on the y-axis. Using this, we can determine that it took Andrew Lauterstein more seconds to finish the 100 metres than the other swimmers. To tell who finished faster between Michael Phelps and Milorad Cavic, however, you will need to look at the second graph. It breaks down the race into 0.2 metre on the x-axis and 0.01 second on the y-axis. With this smaller scale we can see that Phelps won the race, but just barely!

 Phelps won the 100-metre butterfly by a fraction of a centimetre!

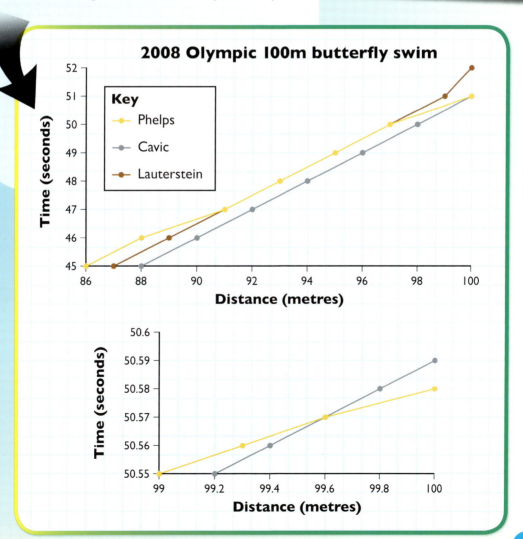

SPORT ON TELEVISION

Since the first televised sporting event in 1931 – the Derby horse race – sport and television have grown hand in hand. All types of sport can be found on television today. There are even channels that only show sport, such as ESPN and Sky Sports.

Sport and advertising

Just as there are many people who watch sport, there are also many companies wanting to advertise to those people. These companies pay large sums of money to put their advertisements on television during major sporting events. In 2007, two sporting events on terrestrial television resulted in advertising success for the commercial channel ITV. The men's Rugby World Cup final in which England played South Africa was watched by on average 15 million people. Lewis Hamilton's attempt to win the Formula 1 championship at the Brazilian Grand Prix was seen by just over 9 million viewers. The two events are thought to have brought in £16 million of advertising revenue. Companies knew that with national interest in each event audience figures would be big. They were therefore willing to pay a lot of money to reach those viewers.

 Golf is now a widely televised sport, with sponsors and tournaments. It has come a long way since its early years.

Instant replay

Many sports now use television recordings to help improve the fairness of their games. These sports use something called instant replay. This means that the game's officials can use television screens to decide how to make close calls. They can use televisions to zoom in, watch in slow motion, and replay a close call as many times as they need to in order to determine the correct decision.

2008 Beijing Olympics on TV

The 2008 Olympic Games were the first to be broadcast in high definition. They were also the most viewed event in television history, with 4.7 billion viewers worldwide (over two-thirds of the world's total population).

Bar graphs

Bar graphs are a good way of comparing numbers against each other. This example compares data on how many television viewers several recent sporting events had. Each event has its own bar. We can see how many millions of viewers each event had by looking at the height of the bar along the y-axis.

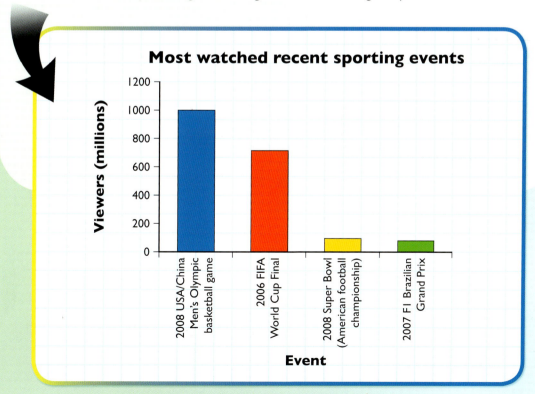

Most watched recent sporting events

Viewers (millions) — y-axis from 0 to 1200

Events (x-axis):
- 2008 USA/China Men's Olympic basketball game
- 2006 FIFA World Cup Final
- 2008 Super Bowl (American football championship)
- 2007 F1 Brazilian Grand Prix

Event

Rugby and **American football** are two of the roughest, toughest sports played. In both games the players take lots of knocks and there is plenty of tackling. They are also fun to play and watch! Let's look at some of the similarities and differences between rugby and American football.

Rugby

The Romans played a game like rugby long ago. However, modern-day rugby was first played in the 1800s in England. It is said that rugby started when a footballer became frustrated because he could only use his feet. In a move that was against the rules he picked up the football and began to run with it. Rugby is now an international success.

American football

American football developed from the English game of rugby. By the late 19th century, American football was played on university campuses across the United States. It is still extremely popular.

Active and healthy

With all the pushing, pulling, running, and kicking in rugby and American football, these sports are great exercise. They burn calories and build muscle!

 A rugby player is being tackled by three players on the opposing team.

	Sport	
	Rugby	**American football**
Developed from?	Football	Rugby
Began in?	Early 19th century	Late 19th century
Championship?	Rugby World Cup	Super Bowl
Amount of protective gear?	Little	Lots
Kicking?	Yes	Yes
Forward passes?	No	Yes
Tackling?	Yes	Yes
Injury rate per 1,000 hours played?	69	35

Giant men

Both professional rugby and American football require lots of strength and athleticism. Many of the players are very large and strong. Recently, the players in both sports have become bigger and stronger than ever. Let's use another bar graph to compare the average weights of professional rugby and American football players to each other. We can also use the bar graph to see how much bigger players from both sports have become over the last 30 years.

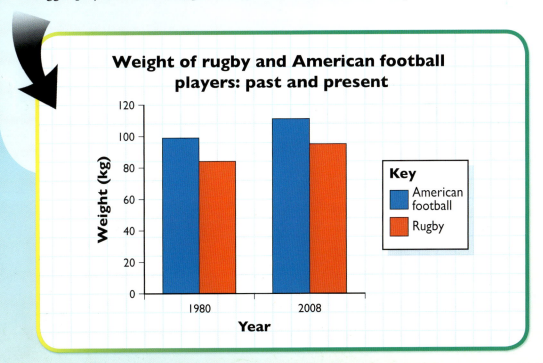

Weight of rugby and American football players: past and present

THE WORLD CUP

In 1930, international football teams from around the world came together in Uruguay for the first ever football World Cup. The World Cup has been held every four years since that time (except in 1942 and 1946 due to World War II). It is the largest, most celebrated, most watched, and most anticipated single sporting event in the world.

 The winners of the World Cup get to celebrate for four years. Below, Italy celebrates their 2006 World Cup victory.

The kings of football

In the three years leading up to the World Cup, many countries compete to be one of the 32 successful teams to play in the tournament. The teams then compete over one month until one team is the winner.

The winner is awarded a trophy. The original trophy was made of gold and silver. It included a figure of Nike, the Greek goddess of victory. This trophy was stolen in 1983 and has never been recovered! A new trophy, the **FIFA** World Cup, is now given to the World Cup winners.

Women's World Cup

The Women's World Cup is also seen as the most important competition in women's football. As with the men's competition, the Women's World Cup takes place every four years. The top 16 teams compete for the trophy over a three-week period.

Continents of dominance

All World Cup championships so far have been won by countries from either Europe or South America. We can use a bar graph to compare how many championships Europe and South America have won. Instead of a regular bar graph, this time we will use a stacked bar graph. A stacked bar graph is special because it not only allows us to compare how many times each continent has won, but it also allows us to see the parts of the whole. This means we can see which countries from each continent have won the World Cup and how many each has won. Can you tell which continent has won the most World Cups? Can you tell which country has won the most?

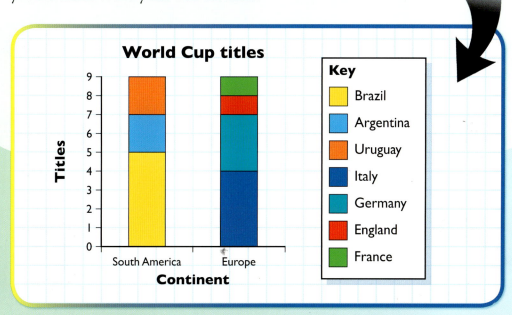

World Cup titles

Key: Brazil, Argentina, Uruguay, Italy, Germany, England, France

SPORTS STADIUMS

Since the beginning of organized sport, teams and spectators have needed a place to compete and watch their favourite sports and teams. The oldest known sports stadium is in Olympia in Greece. This is where the original Olympics were held in 776 BCE. Since that time, sports stadiums have grown larger and the technology used to build and run the stadiums has become more advanced.

Bigger and better

Stadiums built today can sometimes seat over 100,000 people. The Rungrado May Day Stadium in North Korea can seat 150,000 spectators. Some stadiums even include restaurants, hotels, and swimming pools inside.

 Wembley Stadium is a huge complex. It has over 2,600 toilets!

Modern marvels

The technology used at stadiums built today is amazing. Many stadiums have retractable roofs, wireless internet, HDTV screens, and personal monitors. But building huge stadiums with lots of new technology can be very expensive. Stadiums built in China for the 2008 Olympics and those in South Africa for the 2010 World Cup cost their countries over £66 million each.

Wembley Stadium

One of the newest and biggest stadiums is Wembley Stadium in London. It was completed in 2007. It has 90,000 seats and is the most expensive stadium ever built, at nearly £800 million.

Money makers

To pay for the cost of building these huge new stadiums, the stadiums have to make money when they are open for business. Stadiums make their money in three main ways: ticket sales, food and beverage sales, and merchandise sales. To understand the **proportion** of money taken by each way of making money, we need a new type of graph. For this we will use a pie chart. Pie charts are good for looking at how parts make up a whole. We can see how much (what percentage) of the total money a stadium makes comes from each way of making money.

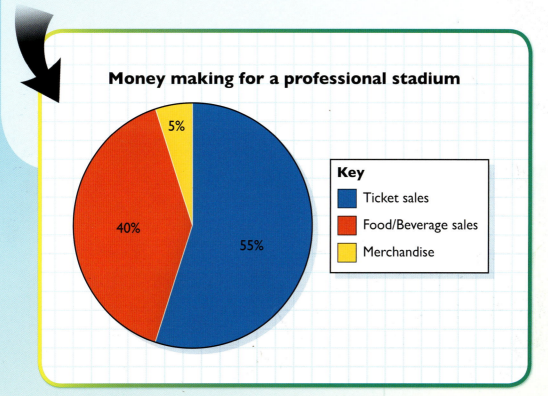

Money making for a professional stadium

5%

40%

55%

Key
- Ticket sales
- Food/Beverage sales
- Merchandise

BOOMING BASKETBALL

Basketball started in a small US town in the late 19th century. It was played using peach baskets, wire backboards, and a football. Whenever one team scored, a stepladder had to be used to get the ball out of the peach basket. Basketball may have started small, but in just over 100 years, it has grown into one of the most popular sports in the United States.

Did you know?

Shaquille O'Neal is one of the greatest basketball players of all time. He has an Olympic gold medal and has won National Basketball Association (NBA) championships. The name Shaquille means "little one" or "little warrior", but Shaquille is one of the biggest men in basketball! You don't have to be big to play basketball, though. Earl Boykins is only 1.65 metres (5 feet, 5 inches) tall and weighs 60 kilograms (133 pounds).

The "little one" stands 2.16 m (7 ft. 1 in.), weighs 147.4 kg (325 lbs), and wears size 22 shoes!

Olympic dominance

Basketball became an official Olympic sport in 1936. From 1936 until 1968, the US basketball team was undefeated in the Olympics, winning seven straight gold medals. However, in 1972, a last-second shot by the Soviet Union in the finals against the US broke the undefeated streak. Since that time, the US has not been as dominant.

Active and healthy
Basketball is great exercise. With all of the running, jumping, shooting, and passing, a person can get in shape and have fun playing basketball.

Scoring trends

There are three ways to score points in basketball. There are 3-point shots. These are shots that come from long range. There are 2-point shots. These are shots made from anywhere inside of the 3-point line. And finally there are free-throws. These are only worth 1 point each and are taken after a foul is committed. To be great at basketball, teams need to be able to score all three ways. Let's use a pie chart to look at how the points were scored by some of the Olympic basketball teams in 2008. The larger the piece of pie is, the more points were scored in that way.

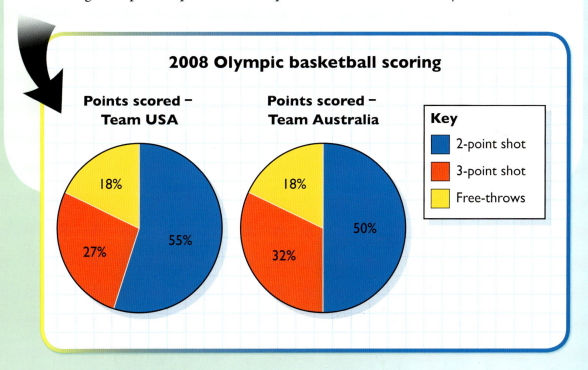

2008 Olympic basketball scoring

Points scored – Team USA
18%
27%
55%

Points scored – Team Australia
18%
32%
50%

Key
- 2-point shot
- 3-point shot
- Free-throws

There are motorcycle races, **NASCAR** races, stock car races, Formula 1 races and many other kinds of races. All motor races have scary speeds, dangerous turns, and death-defying crashes. This excitement is what makes motor racing one of the most popular sports in the world.

Formula 1

Formula 1 (F1) racing is the most popular form of racing in the world. An F1 car can go from 0–160 kph (0–99 mph) and back to 0 kph (0 mph) in only 4 seconds! That is fast, but it is also extremely hard on the engine. Some F1 engines only last about 2 hours before blowing up.

An F1 car races around the track in Finland in 2008. New rules have limited drivers to eight engines per season.

NASCAR

NASCAR is the most popular form of motor racing in the United States. In 1953, a driver named Jim Flock ran his NASCAR races with a monkey on board! During one race while he was in second place, the monkey got loose and Jim had to make a pit stop, which cost him the race.

Active and healthy

Some people may not think that sitting behind the wheel of a car is hard work, but race car driving is not like everyday driving.

Driving a race car can be a lot of work.

◆ The temperature can reach 60 °C (140 °F) inside the car during a race.

◆ A driver can lose 2.2–4.5 kg (5–10 lbs) throughout the course of the race.

◆ Drivers need to drink plenty of water to stay hydrated during a race.

◆ A driver's pulse is at 85 per cent of the maximum rate during the race, similar to that of a marathon runner.

Costly crashes

F1 and NASCAR race cars are made up of thousands of high-tech parts that cost millions of dollars. When these cars crash, they cost a lot of money to repair. Let's look at a special kind of bar graph called a pictograph. This will help us to compare how often these cars crash and how much they cost to repair. This type of graph uses pictures to represent numbers.

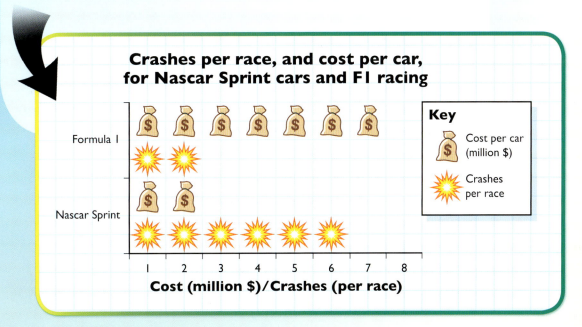

Crashes per race, and cost per car, for Nascar Sprint cars and F1 racing

Cost (million $)/Crashes (per race)

Key
- Cost per car (million $)
- Crashes per race

Hitting a ball with a bat is a popular sport no matter what country you are from. Games using wooden bats and thrown balls have been played for thousands of years all over the world. Most of these games are no longer played, but two bat and ball games thrive. These are **cricket** and **baseball**.

Cricket

The game of cricket was developed hundreds of years ago in England. Each team has 11 players. One team is in the field and the other team bats. There are various forms of cricket played. A game of one-day cricket has one **innings** per team and a game of test cricket has two innings per team. Test cricket can last for a maximum of five days.

Did you know?
A hat trick in cricket is where the bowler dismisses three batsmen or women in consecutive deliveries. It does not happen very often.

 The game of test cricket is played in whites. For one-day games players wear different coloured clothes.

Baseball

Baseball was developed primarily in the United States. Today, the sport of baseball is popular throughout North and South America as well as Asia. Nine players from each team are in the field at a time. Just as in cricket, one team bats while the other is in the field. The game of baseball is played for nine innings but games rarely last more than three or four hours.

The World Baseball Classic is an international baseball tournament that began in 2005. It is played once every four years and allows professional players from all over the world to compete against each other. Even though baseball was invented in the United States, each of the first two World Baseball Classic tournaments has been won by the Japanese team.

Hammerin' Hank 1957 home run distribution

In baseball, the best thing a batter can do is hit a **home run**. This is when the batter hits the ball all the way over the fence without the ball bouncing, similar to hitting a six in cricket. Hank Aaron was one of the best home run hitters of all time. His nickname was Hammerin' Hank because he could really "hammer" the ball hard. Aaron hit home runs in every direction. We can use this special pie chart to help us visualize where Aaron hit most of his home runs.

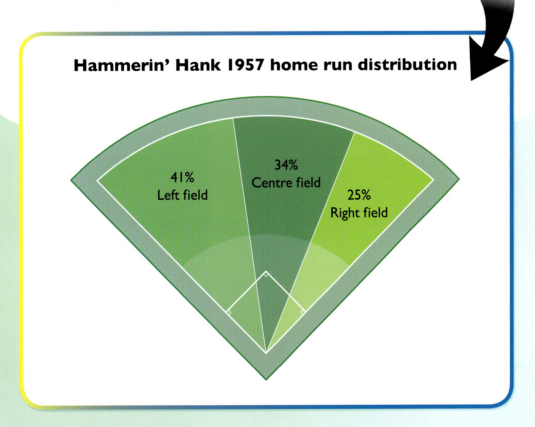

Hammerin' Hank 1957 home run distribution

41% Left field

34% Centre field

25% Right field

THE OLYMPIC GAMES

The largest sporting event in the world today is the Olympic Games. From 776 BCE until 394 CE, the Olympic Games were celebrated in Greece, but they were eventually banned until 1896. Since 1896, the Olympics have grown bigger and bigger. In the 2008 Olympics, a total of 10,500 athletes competed in 302 events. For this, 37 venues had to be used and 12 of these had to be built specially for the Olympics.

Olympic rings

The five rings used to represent the Olympics have a special meaning. The five colours (against the white background) represent the five major regions of the world: Africa, the Americas, Asia, Australia, and Europe. Every national flag in the world includes one of the five colours on the rings. The rings are linked together to represent the countries of the world being linked together in friendship.

Olympic torch

The Olympic torch has been used ever since the ancient Olympic Games in Olympia, Greece. Before each Olympic Games begins, the flame is lit in Olympia using only the sun's rays and mirrors, just like in ancient times. The torch is then carried by runners to the place where the games are held. In 2008, the journey from Olympia to Beijing, China – the site of the 2008 Olympics – was over 137,000 kilometres (85,000 miles) long.

 The 2008 Olympic Games opening ceremony was watched by over 1 billion people.

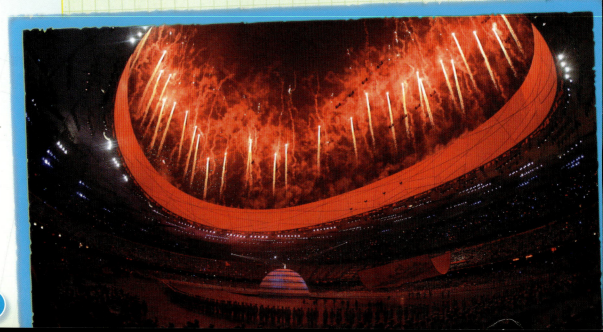

Olympic medals, 2008

We can use a pictograph to compare the number of medals won by some of the countries in the 2008 Olympics. Let's look at the medals won in cycling. In the first graph below, each medal shown represents one medal won. The British team won more gold medals in cycling than all the teams from the rest of the world combined!

The second pictograph shows total gold medals won in 2008 in all sports. This time each medal shown represents five medals won. A partial medal in the graph means somewhere between one and four medals were won. Can you tell how many medals the Chinese team won?

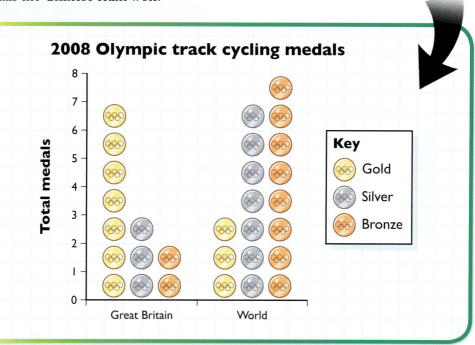

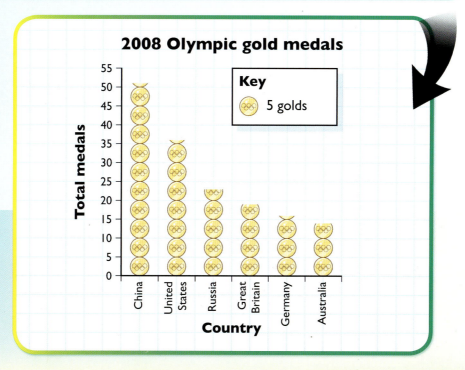

CHART SMARTS

Graphs are a great way to make data easier and more interesting to read. Graphs make comparing data and seeing patterns easier. Any data can be graphed. Graphs can be made with paper and a pencil. Graphs can easily be made on a computer. There are many different types of graphs and each type is best for displaying particular types of data.

Line graphs

Remember the line graph we used to see how Olympic athletes have got faster over time. Line graphs are great for tracking changes over short or long periods of time. Here we tracked 100-metre run finishing times over many years.

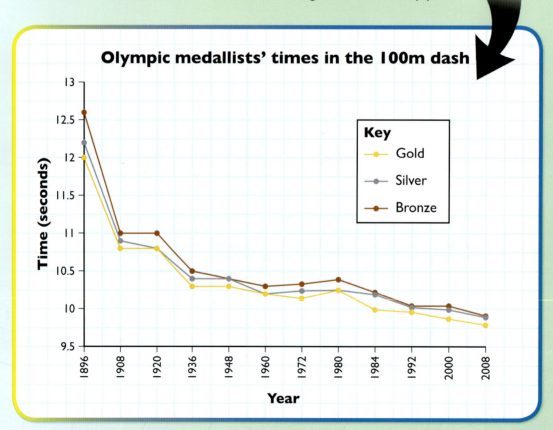

Pie charts

There are three ways to score points in basketball. We used a pie chart to see how much of the total scoring each of the three ways accounted for. Pie charts are great for seeing what proportion of the whole certain parts make up. We used the pie chart to see how much of the total scoring each part – 3-pointers, 2-pointers, and free-throws – made up of the total scoring for the US and Australian basketball teams.

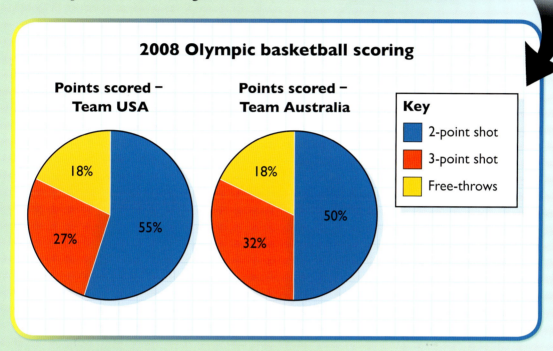

2008 Olympic basketball scoring

Points scored – Team USA

Points scored – Team Australia

Key
- 2-point shot
- 3-point shot
- Free-throws

Team USA: 55%, 27%, 18%
Team Australia: 50%, 32%, 18%

Bar graphs

We used a bar graph to compare the average weight of professional rugby players and professional American footballers. Bar graphs are best for comparing something between two or more different groups. Here we compared weight between two different groups, rugby players and American footballers.

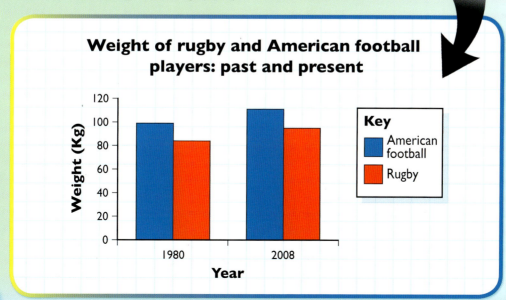

Weight of rugby and American football players: past and present

Weight (Kg) — axis: 0, 20, 40, 60, 80, 100, 120

Year: 1980, 2008

Key
- American football
- Rugby

GLOSSARY

American football a game that developed from rugby that is popular in the United States

baseball a game played with a bat and ball by two teams. The players at bat have to run a course of four bases laid out in a diamond pattern in order to score.

basketball game played between two teams of five players on a court, the object being to throw a ball through an elevated basket on the opponent's side of a rectangular court

cricket game played by two teams of eleven players each with a bat, ball, and two wickets on a pitch. To score, batters have to run between the wickets or hit boundaries (scoring either four or six).

FIFA abbreviation for Fédération Internationale de Football Association, the governing body of international football

home run hit in baseball that allows the batter to make a complete circuit of the diamond and score a run

innings in cricket, the periods of a game during which one team is batting. Innings can also refer to the length of time a batsman or woman has played without getting out. In baseball, an *inning* is one of nine periods of a game, in which each team has a turn at bat.

midfielder footballer whose position is played between the defenders and the forwards

NASCAR abbreviation for National Association for Stock Car Auto Racing, a type of racing popular in the United States

paralympic athlete who competes in the Paralympic Games, an international athletic competition for athletes with disabilities

proportion size of a group of data compared to other groups, or to the whole set of data

rugby game played by two teams of 13 to 15 players each on a rectangular field, the object being to run with an oval ball across the opponent's goal line or kick it through the upper portion of goal posts

track and field group of sports that include running, jumping, and throwing events

water polo sport played in the water where two teams compete to pass a ball into the other's goal

World Cup most important football tournament in the world. Thirty-two international teams compete in it every four years.

x-axis horizontal axis of a two-dimensional graph

y-axis vertical axis of a two-dimensional graph

FURTHER INFORMATION

Books

Football (Dorling Kindersley, 2008)

Know Your Sport (series) (Franklin Watts, 2006)

Modern Olympic Games, Haydn Middleton (Heinemann Library, 2008)

Sport Files (series) (Heinemann Library, 2008)

Sports Science: Cycling, James Bow (Franklin Watts, 2009)

Sports Science: Swimming, Hélène Boudreau (Franklin Watts, 2009)

Websites

Learn about different types of graphs with these factsheets.
http://www.bbc.co.uk/skillswise/numbers/handlingdata/graphs_and_charts/factsheet.shtml

Youth Sport Trust is a charity that aims to increase and improve children's participation in sport.
http://www.mrnussbaum.com/coolgraphing.htm

This is the site for the UK School Games, a four-day event that tries to copy the atmosphere and arrangement of major events such as the Olympics.
http://www.ukschoolgames.com/

This is the official Olympic Games website. You can find lots of information about the Games and can even search for Olympic medal-winners since 1896.
http://www.olympic.org/uk/games/index_uk.asp

Place to visit

Wembley Stadium
Wembley
London
HA9 0WS
www.wembleystadium.com/default.aspx

INDEX